Wood

Sustainability
Versatility
Stability

Works

118 Klein A45
122 Arosa
126 Tower House
132 Edel:Weiss Residences
136 Branched Offices
140 Weingarthaus
144 Courmayeur
146 Boundary House
148 Elephant Park
149 From Stable to Passive House
150 FLEXSE
154 SM House
158 House with Cherry Tree
162 Blue Bottle South Park
166 Dome of Visions 3.0
170 Outdoor Areas Palais Thermal
172 House Felder
176 La Bohème Entre Amis
178 Casa GG
182 Baumhaus Halden
186 National Museum of Qatar
    Gift Shops
192 Øvre Tomtegate 7
196 Fazenda Boa Vista
200 Bookshelf House
206 Pano Brot & Kaffee
210 Gamsei Cocktail Bar
214 Pedersen Residence
220 Index
222 Picture Credits

Preface

Wood is an extremely versatile building material – both in application and in appearance. Although it always shows its natural origin (p. 24), it can also appear completely artificial when softly deformed (p. 14) or used in the most stringent of geometries (p. 210). Hard bends and edges (p. 18) are feasible and surfaces that – across boards – appear precisely like steel (p. 178). But wood can also be used to create natural formations that make no secret of their artificiality (p. 186). The lightweight but robust building material makes it possible to create unusual shapes (p. 71) and can be adapted quickly, easily and inexpensively to a wide variety of applications.

By using different wood finishes, individual areas can be separated from one another (p. 172). Diverse textures (p. 8) or different woods (p. 30) as well as old woods (p. 35) create very different impressions. For example, the impression of a conglomerate can be sought which nevertheless appears uniform in the overarching material wood (p. 214). The collection of historical wooden cases in the Modern Dandy apartment (p. 39) is a particularly original example of this. The wooden wine boxes have a similar function in the design of La Galerie du Vin (p. 57).

The combination of boards or beams makes it easy to create patterns and rhythmic sequences – both on a small scale (p. 34) and on a large scale (p. 133). But the material also has its own pattern, the grain, which provides variety in the surface, even if the boards themselves form a uniform row (p. 48). The individual grain of the material always leads to unique pieces (p. 145) or to a kind of surface decoration (p. 107), and the alignment of boards makes it possible to overdraw distances (p. 65) or connect different zones (p. 197). Different shades of wood often play well together (p. 162) and the change in color of aging wood can also be used as an esthetic moment (p. 192). In combination with other materials, wood can create a raw impression (p. 91), can loosen up a strict minimalism (p. 93), or continue an "as found" esthetic (p. 97). Wood is both majestic enough to serve sacred purposes (p. 101) and unpretentious enough for school buildings (p. 105) or even supposed to appear as an inexpensive material (p. 119). The different color and brightness values make it possible to create very different situations: from hermetic (p. 147) to airy (p. 166).

In most cases, wood inevitably refers to traditional building techniques, but this reference can also be emphasized in the design, be it wood shingle (p. 75) or half-timbered (p. 61). This is also where bamboo construction comes in as a special area of timber construction (p. 79). The stud construction method also picks up on historical models and leads them to something new (p. 137), while the tree house (p. 182) becomes a modern hideaway.

Wood conveys an informal working atmosphere (p. 20), stands for closeness to nature (p. 141) and serves as a reference to craftsmanship (p. 206). In the furnishings, wood provides a natural appearance (p. 83). Especially in the living environment, it is an excellent material for fixtures (p. 127). Since wood can characterize both building construction and furnishings, extremely homogeneous designs are possible (p. 158), with static elements merging into the furniture (p. 200). In regions with a pronounced timber construction radius, timber is often found in residential construction (p. 26), and traditional building types are also often transformed into modern interiors (p. 123).

The construction can also be made of wood and be conspicuous as such (p. 43) or of another material (p. 44). In battens and claddings, wood can stretch across any shape and thus form very uniform surfaces across edges (p. 170) or unite volumes (p. 115). Wooden constructions can be extremely filigree (p. 52) and allow large spans and thus large glazing areas (p. 85) and projections (p. 154). The wooden construction of the Elephant Park in Zurich (p. 56) or La Bohème Entre Amis (p. 176), for example, can be used as a means of expression.

Last but not least, wood is an ecological building material. Renewable and available locally almost everywhere (p. 111), it is not only extremely environmentally friendly but also shows this at first glance (p. 149). It is completely recyclable (p. 150) and binds carbon dioxide.

Architect/designer: Olson Kundig

Location: Winthrop, WA, USA
Completion: 2012
Building type: house

Studhorse

Varying tones of salvaged wood siding reveal the history and use of Studhorse.

Set in the remote Methow Valley, Studhorse responds to the clients' desire to experience and interact with the surrounding environment throughout all four seasons. Riffing on the tradition of circling wagons, the buildings – four small, unattached structures – are scattered around a central courtyard and pool offering carefully composed views of the surrounding Studhorse Ridge Mountains and Pearrygin Lake. Traditional boundaries between the built structures and their surroundings are purposefully blurred. The design is oriented toward family life and entertaining. Public areas, including the family room, kitchen and bar, are grouped together in the main building. Private areas are separated in an adjacent structure, with guest rooms in yet another isolated building to allow for independent use. A sauna sits removed from the cluster of activity with a framed view looking out over the valley below. The wood siding used throughout the project was salvaged from an old barn.

Architect/designer: Innarch

Location: Prishtina, Kosovo
Completion: 2013
Building type: café

Don Café

The bar shape refers to the design of the seating areas, while the organic shaped modules function as both an esthetic feature and a structural organization element.

The starting point for this café was the wish to offer customers the opportunity to taste the products in the new environments of the Don Café house in a series of chain coffeehouses set up across Kosovo and beyond. Innarch's inspiration derives from sacks filled with coffee grains. The walls of the bar are organically shaped and have the same color as sacks of coffee, while the pillars in between are coated with textile coffee sacks. Tables and hanging chandeliers represent the coffee grains lined up asymmetrically in order to give the impression of being inside a coffee sack. For the purposes of generating the organic shape, the plywood material was formed using CNC machines and the parts were then assembled.

Architect/designer: MOD

Location: Tianjin, China
Completion: 2011
Building type: gallery

Vanke Triple V Gallery

MOD's dramatic design for the Triple V Gallery has become an icon along the Dong Jiang Bay coastline. Designed as a permanent show gallery and tourist information center for Vanke, China's largest developer, the building's design evolved rationally from a careful analysis of key contextual and programmatic factors. The tourist center and the show gallery are oriented to separate pedestrian pathways and can be operated independently. Discussions are conducted in the lounge area. Tectonically, the building responds to the coastal setting and is finished in weather-sensitive Corten steel panels on its exterior and timber strips on the interior walls and ceiling.

Architect/designer: +ADD

Location: New York City, NY, USA
Completion: 2014
Building type: work space

FiftyThree, Inc.

Defined by walnut wood, concrete, blackened steel and glass, this workspace is a combination between office, home, library and forest.

FiftyThree is a space to create – a combination between work space, library, home, restaurant and forest. Under the creed "honest materials and understated confidence", the architects created a space that involves an honest and open layout promoting teamwork and all forms of collaboration. The selection of materials: walnut wood, blackened steel, glass, and concrete complemented by marble accents became the palette for the design. The wood platforms in the center of the space consist of an elevated space that has the function of gathering the whole team for weekly meetings or announcements, but also to have one-to-one brainstorming sessions. The architects strongly believed that by changing the spatial perception they could also trigger different behaviors and approaches to the regular meeting experience.

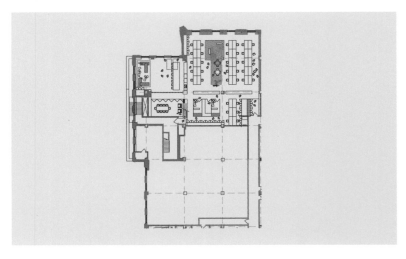

Architect/designer: Partisans

Location: Lake Huron, Canada
Completion: 2014
Building type: sauna

Grotto Sauna

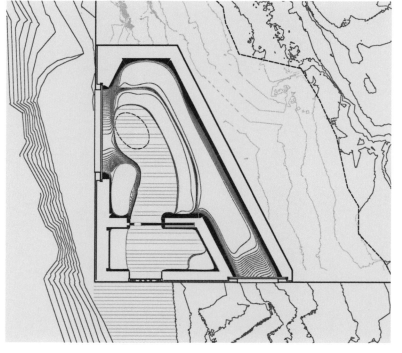

Perched at the northwest edge of an island in Georgian Bay, Grotto Sauna is an example of old-world craftsmanship and new-world sustainability made possible by cutting-edge software and fabrication technology. It is a sculpted space, a sensual experience, and a sophisticated exercise in building science. Inspired by an Italian grotto the design pays homage to the extremities of the Northern Ontario landscape. A simple but dignified exterior built from charred cedar prepared using the traditional Japanese Shu Sugi Ban method conveys a weathered appearance – it's as if the building has been hidden in plain sight for centuries. By contrast, the warm, curved interior emulates Lake Huron's waves and mirrors the Precambrian shield – a soft, undulating rock surface that has been worn down over billions of years.

Architect/designer: Jachen Könz architetto

Location: Montagnola, Switzerland
Completion: 2009
Building type: apartment building

Casa Camar

A well-organized apartment structure combining functionality with individual comfort.

Casa Camar is an apartment building comprising four residential units that develop in a staggered arrangement over four levels. The shape and position of the building were defined by the plot boundaries. Wall elements facing the street modulate a row of concave rooms that all feature large windows and openings in order to effectively mediate between interior and exterior. The apartments are all organized over two levels with the bedrooms below and kitchen and living area above. The staggered arrangement makes it possible for more light to be drawn inside via the roof terrace to the southwest. The apartments are oriented towards the north, which makes optimal use of the views over the landscape.

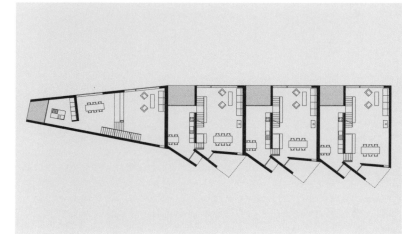

Architect/designer: Reiulf Ramstad Arkitekter

Location: Ål, Norway
Completion: 2013
Building type: cottage

V-Lodge

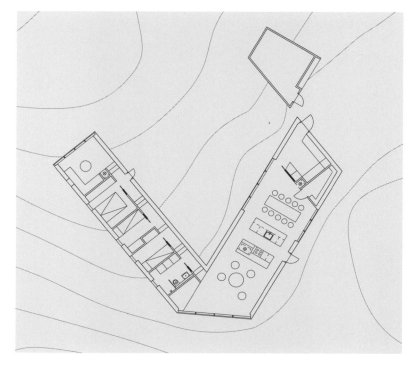

A perfect place for wintery relaxation where you cannot only see, but feel the nature.

This cabin, suitable for use all year round, is located in the mountains above the village of Ål in Buskerud, nestled amidst tracks used for cross-country skiing in winter and hiking in summer. The structure responds to the existing topography and natural surroundings, while taking advantage of the site's natural benefits. In its form, program and materials, the lodge is characterized by simplicity and a strong relationship to the surroundings. The building consists of two bodies united in a V-shaped plan with a south-facing glazed wall at its chamfered intersection. The main body accommodates the entrance hall and combined dining, kitchen and living zones, oriented to echo the site's natural contours. The second body contains a bathroom, three bedrooms and a youth lodge at the far end, each on stepped levels in alignment with the falling terrain. The exterior walls and pitched roofs are clad entirely in pre-patinated heart pine, providing a homogenous skin that blends with its surroundings.

Architect/designer: sistémica

Location: Mexico City, Mexico
Completion: 2014
Building type: wine shop

Boutique Intersybarite

This small retail space sells only the best gourmet products that also take center stage in the design, becoming an eye-catching attraction within a showroom-like setting. This project is the result of a desire to achieve an intriguing and visually striking atmosphere, with the cellar devised as a key element of the design concept. The space is open to the public, stirring the curiosity of passersby and drawing visitors inside. The wood used was recycled from used pallets, which not only gives the design a unique feel, but also helped to reduce cost and environmental impact.

Architect/designer: AATA Architects
(Nicole Gardilcic and Sebastián Cerda)

Location: Hanga Roa, Easter Island, Chile
Completion: 2010
Building type: holiday cottages

Morerava Cottages

Developing the tourist complex of the Morerava Cabins on Easter Island, the architects' motivation for creating family-friendly cabins that meet certain quality standards and correspond to the context of the island by minimizing its impact on it led them to the decision to execute the prefabrication on the continent and then ship the material to the island. Other aspects minimizing the intervention in the natural terrain are the single pillars that preserve natural water absorption and the conservation of local plants and shrubs that have been integrated into the overall design and ambience.

Architect/designer: Mork-Ulnes Architects /sfosl

Location: Sebastopol, CA, USA
Completion: 2015
Building type: house and atelier

Meier Road

The project began with the design of several new structures on the couple's 12,140-square-meter farm: an unusual estate that exemplifies the creative spontaneity and penchant for experimentalism of the owners and their architect. The catalyst and primary inspiration for the project was the desire to invigorate an old, derelict barn on the rural property located in Sebastopol with new life. Using the barn typology had an instant appeal. The main challenge was the creation of the ideal art studio within the barn vernacular. A 66.9-square-meter kitchen and dining space now grows out from the studio. Nicknamed the "Amoeba", it offers a loose and organic counterpoint to the more rigorous barn structure from which it extends.

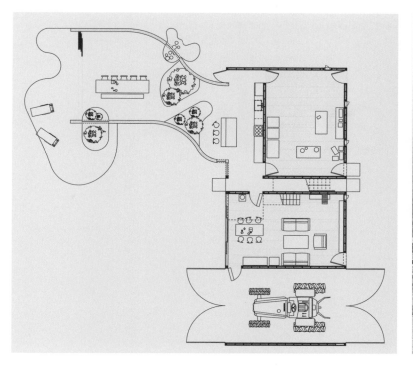

An old barn turned into a modern complex where creativity and art function as driving forces.

Architect/designer: Goodnova Godiniaux with Yulia Orlova

Location: Moscow, Russia
Completion: 2013
Building type: apartment

Modern Dandy

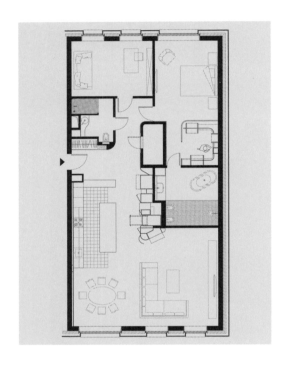

This unusual apartment is designed with a globetrotter in mind, a perpetual traveler who nevertheless decided to set down his suitcases in Moscow. Inspired by the idea of travel and by the esthetic qualities of light, the design welcomes natural light into the space and allows it to flow freely through the living areas, a symbolic echo of the client's free-flowing nature. A central module concentrates all of the main functions, separates the rooms from each other, reduces the amount of furniture required and allows the space to break free from the constraints of corridors. Clad in a single material (mutene timber), it provides continuity and consistency while the rooms that cluster around it each have their own unique esthetic.

The idea of travel serves as source of inspiration for this extraordinary apartment.

Architect/designer: Tank architectes

Location: Proville, France
Completion: 2008
Building type: library

Library in Proville

The wooden clad will age with time, providing the library with a changing and individual appearance.

The Library in Proville was designed to be a library and a place of cultural and social exchange for the inhabitants of the village of Proville, France. The building has a metallic frame clad in wood designed to turn gray as it ages. Natural light is admitted through large aluminum-framed windows, which also take advantage of the natural heat supplied by the sun. A terrace on the roof can be used as an outdoor reading space. Inside, a series of uniquely designed spaces offer a variety of atmospheres and lighting effects. Partitions, patios and niches have been incorporated to provide a range of spatial experiences.

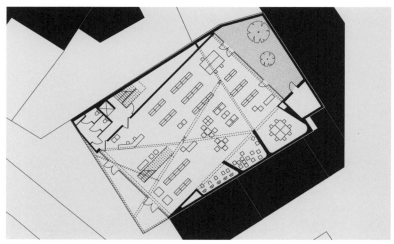

Architect/designer: Tham & Videgård Arkitekter

Location: Krokholmen, Värmdö, Sweden
Completion: 2015
Building type: holiday home

House Krokholmen

The clients wanted a maintenance-free vacation home in one level with social space both inside and outside. The large family room with kitchen and entrance faces out towards the sea with daylight and view in three directions. A central wall holding the fireplace gives access to bedrooms, bath and storage that are oriented to the forest in the west. The living room opens up through large sliding doors onto three terraces. The tent-like silhouette of the house connects to the idea of the least complicated way to spend time in nature, but it is also inspired by the older Swedish pavilion – and gazebo architecture, light buildings carefully placed in the landscape. A screen of wood and glass runs around the house and unites interior and exterior spaces on a base of in-situ cast concrete.

A tent-like structure that is inspired by the surrounding nature, underlined by soft wooden tones and a clear formal language.

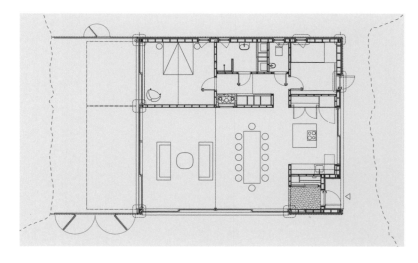

Architect/designer: HB Architecture

Location: Tongariro National Park, New Zealand
Completion: 2011
Building type: café

Knoll Ridge Café

Timber has been used extensively to create a warm traditional mountain chalet feeling.

Knoll Ridge Café is located at Whakapapa Skifield on Mount Ruapehu in the Tongariro National Park, New Zealand. Situated on the side of a mountain, the commercial ski field is located on New Zealand's largest active volcano. Rapidly changing weather is typical for the conditions encountered in this area. The café has to withstand wind speeds of up to 200 kilometers per hour and temperatures well below freezing. In the summer season the eastern face of the building can be seen set above the volcanic rock formations. Timber has been used extensively to create the warm atmosphere connected with a mountain chalet without adopting the traditional form. The glass exterior is a significant feature, allowing guests to have a coffee whilst enjoying the magnificent views of Pinnacle Ridge. To meet the various requirements, the staff facilities and public sanitary facilities are situated in a separate external area.

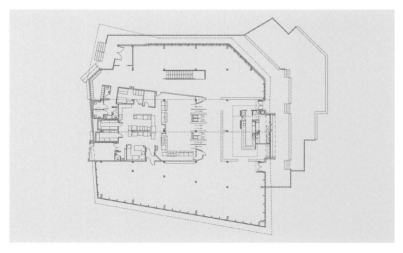

Architect/designer: OOS

Location: Zurich, Switzerland
Completion: 2010
Building type: wine store

La Galerie du Vin

La Galerie du Vin serves as sales, tasting and seminar space that appeals to both customers and passersby alike. The design concept by OOS responds to the company's values and traditions, placing the wine itself at the center of the design. The walls are covered with around 1,500 wine crates from the Bordeaux region, giving the space an almost grotto-like character. Organized into a platform, these crates accommodate approximately 570 wine bottles, as well as serving as illuminated tables and seating elements. A reception counter is located in the center of the room; its violet and ruby colors create a striking contrast to the light wood of the wine crates.

By using wooden wine crates to cover the walls and ceiling a distinctive and yet functional design has been created.

Architect/designer: Tailored design Lab.

Location: Ishikawa, Japan
Completion: 2011
Building type: residential renovation

House Refurbish-ment in Kaga

A place of personal memory
to live in silence, harmony and
peaceful surroundings.

The 70-year-old client wanted a renovation of his 70-year-old house that would evoke memories of an earlier home, matching its beauty and its ambience. The ground floor space, originally used for large village gatherings and ceremonies, has been remodeled as a more intimate Doma space for meeting close friends and family. The new Doma is a "subtraction", according to the designers, a symbol of purity. By carefully stripping the wood from the ceiling joists, a large double-height space that uncovers the building's basic structure was created, revealing the robust roof trusses above. The wood, finished with an elegant traditional red stain, is repurposed from the ceiling to the ground floor as floorboards, tabletops, and handrails. To complete the Doma, the ground floor's original soil was solidified and a window added high above.

Architect/designer: studio mk27
Landscape architect: Consuelo Grossi Pereira

Location: Campo de Jordão, Brazil
Completion: 2015
Building type: house

Casa Mororó

Casa Mororó was designed by Marcio Kogan, Maria Cristina Motta and Diana Radomysler of studio mk27 and is located in a mountainous region, 180 kilometers from the city of São Paulo, known for its low temperatures. The architecture sought to create generous internal spaces for cold days, including a cozy living room and an enclosed bathhouse with a pool. Externally, the same continuous volume creates a duality between an opaque block with the living room, bedrooms and service areas, and the heated pool and sauna with their transparent envelope. An external wooden deck connects the spaces and creates a solarium to be used during the summer months. In the opaque part of the volume, which is 50 meters long, the openings were minimized and used as sliding doors to intensify the integration between inside and outside.

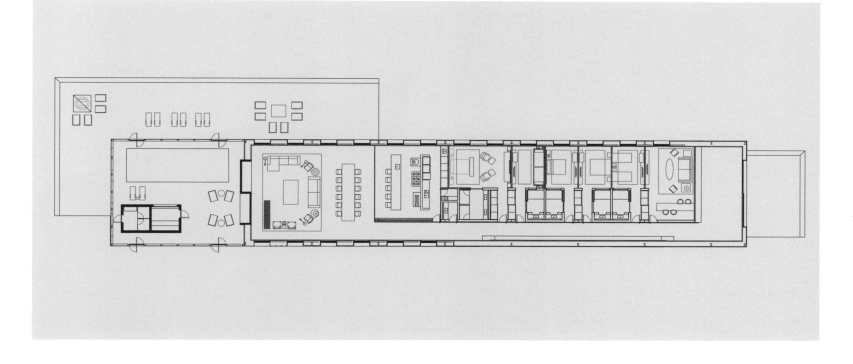

The cozy ambience generates
a welcome warmth in the chilly
mountain region.

Architect/designer: ALA Architects

Location: Kristiansand, Norway
Completion: 2011
Building type: arts center, concert hall

Kilden Performing Arts Centre

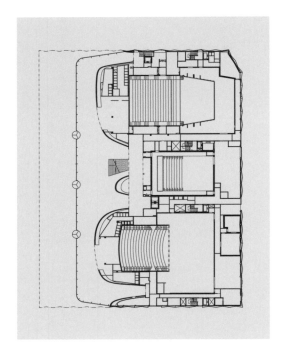

The Kilden Performing Arts Centre, completed in 2011 in Kristiansand, Norway, brings together all the region's performing arts institutions. Kristiansand Symphony Orchestra boasts a 1,200-seat concert hall. The theater group performs in a 700-seat theater that can be transformed to accommodate opera performances by the local opera ensemble. In addition, there is a stage for experimental theater and a multipurpose hall. Kilden promotes experiences; the monumental abstract form of the wooden front façade separates reality from fantasy. Passing through, the audience moves from a natural landscape to the realm of performing arts. The black of the other three façades emphasizes the spectacle of the foyer. The project was executed using mostly local materials, and follows the original design plan.

The Kilden Performing Arts Centre meets the requirements of an ensemble dedicated to human creativity.

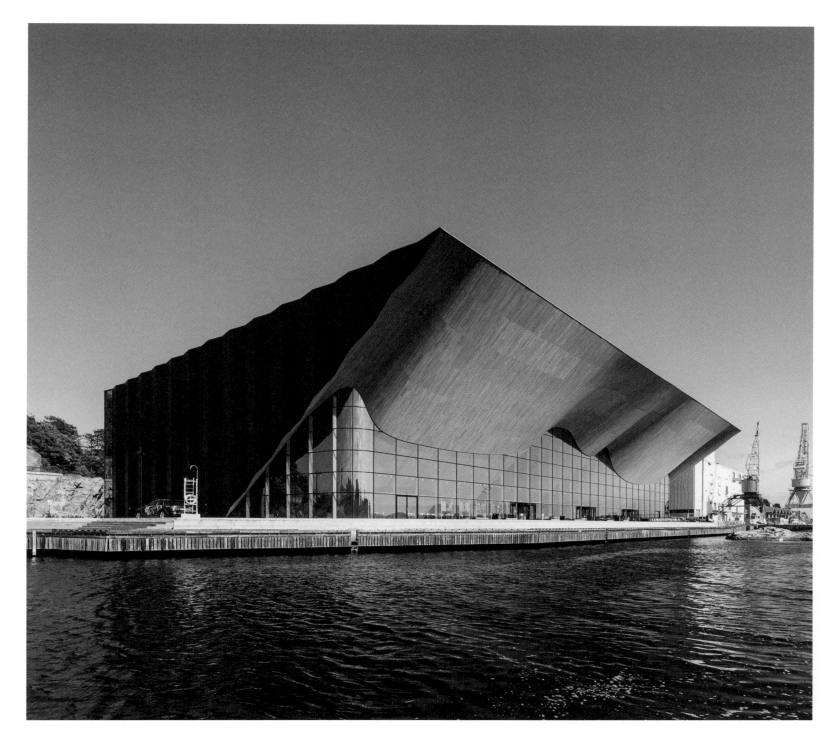

Architect/designer: bergmeisterwolf Architekten   Location: Lajen, Italy
Completion: 2012
Building type: wood carving

Holzschnitzerei Perathoner

For this design, wood was used as the most important esthetic element instead of being limited to the role of a sustainable building material.

This new build was designed to evoke the long tradition of Grödner handicraft and the wood on which it depends. The process of manipulating wood is at the heart of the design. The façade features the same visual and textural irregularities found in wood, presenting itself as a vast wooden sculpture. This impression is strengthened by the irregular aging of the shingle. The self-supporting folding system composed of triangles, accentuated by the surrounding gutter as a shadow gap, can also be sensed and experienced in the interior. There is just one section of steel framework in this pure wood structure; at this juncture, the façade is fully glazed to enable the greatest possible amount of light to enter the exhibition space.

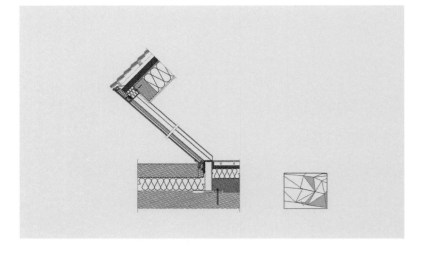

Architect/designer: Luz de Piedra

Location: Puerto Jimenez, Costa Rica
Completion: 2011
Building type: holiday home

Atrevida House

The symbiosis of bamboo and concrete combines tradition with modernity.

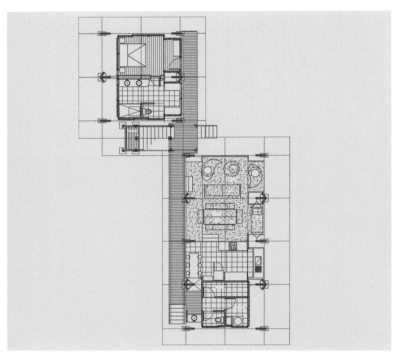

The design of the house is bold and its open character gives its residents the desired sense of freedom. Built by using Guadua bamboo, the house is two stories in height and designed to withstand earthquakes. It has been built on a high concrete base, which helps to protect and isolate the bamboo from water. The design cleverly encourages cross ventilation, while the open areas and large windows have the additional advantage of drawing a wealth of light inside. A system on the roof provides energy for heating water, reinforcing the eco-friendly character of the entire design. The house clearly responds to its surroundings: The wide wooden supports, the use of bamboo and wood and the openness of the ground floor in contrast to the more solid second floor all deliberately evoke the idea of a group of trees in a forest.

Architect/designer: Rever & Drage Architects

Location: Stavanger, Norway
Completion: 2013
Building type: house extension

Feisteinveien

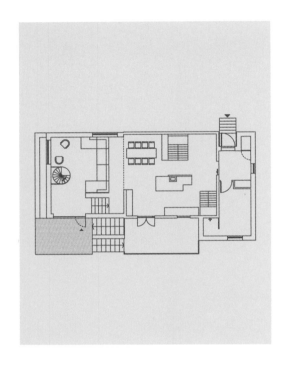

The contrasting colors give the new volume an independent character.

This extension to a single-family house in Stavanger was made to make room for a growing family in a city which has increasingly developed over the last decades due to the economic boom related to the area's oil industry. The large extension to the north contains two small bedrooms on the upper floor, a living room at ground level, and a combined home cinema and exercise room in the basement. The two bedrooms are reached by a winding staircase connected at the top by a glass platform and stairs leading to the roof terrace. The small extension to the south contains bathroom and main entrance.

Architect/designer: Bates Masi + Architects

Location: Southampton, NY, USA
Completion: 2012
Building type: house

Far Pond

Wet and wild! This striking design makes the most of views over the wetlands.

The waterfront site overlooks layers of wetlands and offers views over the estuary, bay, and the ocean. The existing house was built in the 1970s, and the client expressed a wish to maintain the existing structure while doubling the size of the house with an extension. The existing house clearly expressed the structural system, and it was decided that the extension should also do this. The new system utilizes prefabricated elements that resolve multiple structural and spatial problems. Reducing the use of structural components minimized construction waste.

Vigoss R&D

Organic curves create a distinctive design that is determined by elegance and roughness.

This space, designed by Zemberek Design team Başak Emrence, Şafak Emrence and Ece Ilgın Avcı, is a studio within the headquarters of a textile company. The design concept is based on the physical relations among the users, products, accessories, and the materials. The concept is based on the idea of establishing a platform that can accommodate a range of processes and ways of working, instead of using a desk, which only offers a limited usable area. The designers have created a flexible office space where one can sit or stand, move around and easily access other areas of the complex. The curvilinear form supports fluent and flexible movement. The use of just a few main materials makes it easier for employees to concentrate on the products and the tasks at hand rather than being continually distracted.

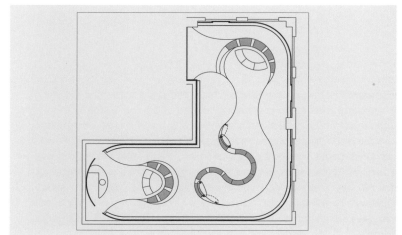

Architect/designer: Architekten
Wannenmacher + Möller

Location: Dusseldorf, Germany
Completion: 2011
Building type: house

Residence in Dusseldorf

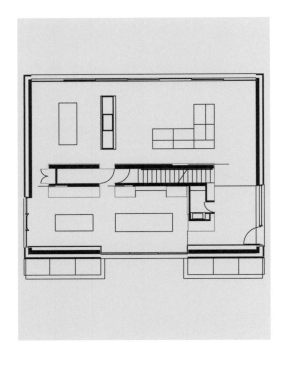

This house is located in one of the most beautiful residential areas of Dusseldorf. The estate was first developed under the National Socialist regime from 1935 to 1936 in connection with an exhibition designed to celebrate the domestic accomplishments of the government. The estate, comprising 95 whitewashed brick houses, constituted the southeastern end of the former exhibition area and is located close to the Rhine river. It served as the prime example of a National Socialist colony for artists and workers. All of the houses were built according to a prototype and, with their rural character, corresponded to the National Socialist building guidelines.

A simple design uniting classic forms and dynamic contrasts to create a clear and transparent living environment.

Architect/designer: Alvaro Moragrega / Arquitecto

Location: Tapalpa, Mexico
Completion: 2018
Building type: house

Casa BGS

Stone, wood and spacious openings melt to create a clear but distinctive design.

Casa BGS consists of two small cabins connected by a living area in the middle of the Tapalpa forest. Each cabin consists of a simple two-story stone building with several openings. The stone composition is demarcated with Douglas fir framing each door and window, resulting in a pattern reminiscent of Mondrian's simplest paintings. The bath is conceived as a space to be inhabited instead of just being utilitarian. The black granite floor contrasts the metallic bathtub. The shower is located outside the stone cabin within a wooden enclosure and topped by a glass skylight that allows for a view of the surrounding pine forest. The whole bath area is clad in wood, including the ceiling which consists of two layers functioning as support of the hardwood floor of the second sleeping area. The lighting design comprises direct installations above the wooden surfaces, as well as chandeliers made of hanging fabric cables. All the plumbing is exposed in copper and bronze to express a sense of sculptural quality.

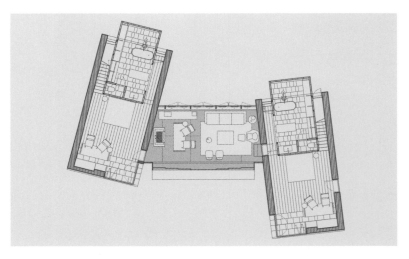

Architect/designer: Tsushima Design Studio

Location: Hangzhou, Zhejiang, China
Completion: 2010
Building type: church

Mei Li Zhou Church

Located in a wooded development in Hangzhou, China, the Mei Li Zhou Church was designed to blend with the surrounding natural landscape and also to act as a space in which all members of the local community would feel welcome and at home. The main chapel is one of several buildings that comprise the church and is entered via a broad stairway leading to the triangular façade. Inside, the rising slant of the triangular ceiling engulfs the lightly finished vertical walls. A solid white floor contrasts the dark wood above. The smaller courtyard office and garden chapel are constructed mainly from stone, tiles and rendered walls, while a tall stone bell tower completes the architectural grouping.

The wooden cladding creates a warm interior that welcomes all members of the local community and serves as modest frame for its spiritual purpose.

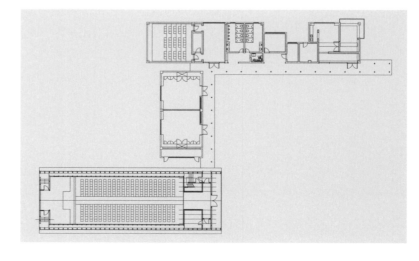

Architect/designer: Raimund Dickinger /
Mario Ramoni

Location: Haid, Austria
Completion: 2011
Building type: college

Agricultural College Ritzlhof

Raimund Dickinger and Mario Ramoni have designed a new annex for an agricultural school in Austria, where 600 students study every year. The new structure includes an entrance to the complex and links existing buildings with an underground corridor. An atrium and multipurpose hall are housed in the center of the interior, while teaching rooms, a library, a foyer and a cloakroom are arranged around this core space. The filigree wood structure, designed in the style of a pavilion, rests on an exposed concrete foundation. The architects followed a similar architectural style to the existing buildings, which include a landmarked residential building from the early 20th century.

Architect/designer:: UID architects – Keisuke Maeda

Location: Onomichi, Japan
Completion: 2010
Building type: house

Nest

A sheltered nest for its residents that pays homage to the subtleties of nature.

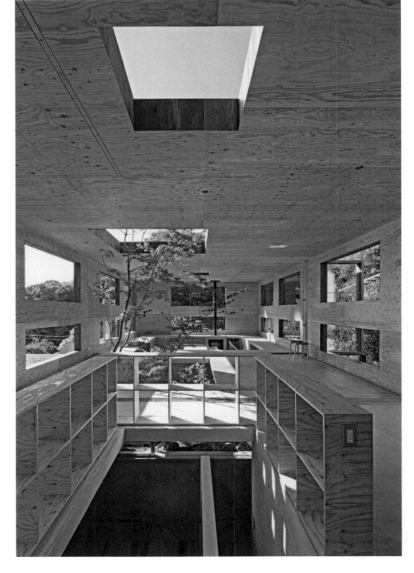

This small house was built in a forest surrounded by rich nature. The site is located at the foot of a mountain with a few scattered neighboring houses in Onomichi, Hiroshima. The ensemble is characterized by a harmonious relationship between the site's environment and its architecture. Inspired by the nests formed by creatures in the nearby forests, the architects aimed to generate a dwelling that was a continuation of its surroundings. With this design a single space was created that connects with the surroundings by rethinking fundamental elements such as floors and walls. On the ground floor spaces are connected with each other via a tunnel that becomes a concrete anthill with a small entrance. Above the ground a floating wooden nest box composed of elements such as branches and fallen leaves cover the nest.

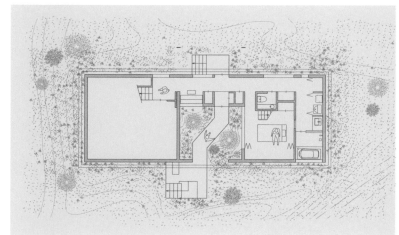

Architect/designer: Tyin Tegnestue Architects

Location: Møre og Romsdal, Norway
Completion: 2016
Building type: cottage

K21 Skardsøya

The spruce wood used for the exterior cladding was harvested from the client's own forest.

This cottage combines important aspects of Norwegian cultural history with the amenities of a modern living space. The structure is modest in size and surrounded by marshland, rocks close to the sea and scattered pine and juniper vegetation. The main building is a stud house with beamed ceilings on three different levels. Most of the construction work was carried out by the owners themselves. The outside of the building is covered with spruce, which was harvested from the clients' own forest. The interior is dominated by light wood and soft tones that contrast the roughness of the surrounding nature and adapt the principles of traditional Norwegian design to combine them with contemporary eye-catchers.

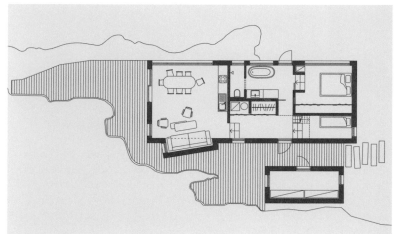

Architect/designer: Rossetti + Wyss Architekten

Location: Horgen, Switzerland
Completion: 2012
Buildng type: detached house

Gottshalden

A compendium of impressions
gleaming inside through its warm
wooden structures.

Villa Gottshalden is located high on a plateau overlooking Lake Zurich. The lush green surroundings are extremely fertile and used for agriculture. The freestanding structure is simple, defined by its wooden materiality and angular form. A wooden shell envelops the façades and roof, providing a uniform materiality across the exterior surface. The structure is comprised of different geometric shapes, while the windows, sitting flush with the façades, are supported by bright interior soffits. The L-shaped plan is organized into several split-level spaces that are bound together by the oak flooring that forms a continuum throughout the interior. The static design is premised on the particular qualities of the oak, which has superb load-bearing capacities and removes the need for concrete reinforcements. Together with the concrete walls, the oak floorboards provide esthetic continuity and generate a sense of warmth that counteracts the structure's angular geometry and white interior surfaces.

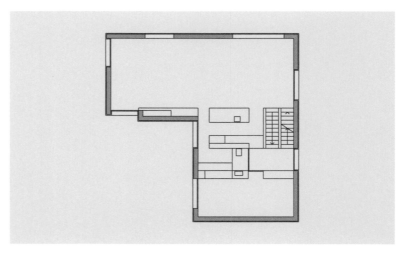

Architect/designer: BIG-Bjarke Ingels Group for Klein House

Location: New York, USA
Completion: 2018
Building type: tiny house

Klein A45

This design evolves from the traditional A-frame cabin, known for its pitched roof and angled walls which allow for easy rain run-off and simple construction. The interior space reflects a minimal Nordic abode prioritized for "hyggelig" comfort. With the exposed timber frame in solid pine, the Douglas fir floor and customizable space-grade, insulating natural cork walls, Klein A45 brings nature inside. An elegant wood-burning fireplace is nestled in one corner while off-the-grid equipment is tucked away in the back. A small kitchen, furniture and bed are some of the handcrafted Nordic design elements to adorn the project. The bathroom is made of cedar wood and consists of 100 percent recyclable materials including the timber frame, wall modules, a subfloor and the triangular floor-to-ceiling window allowing natural daylight to illuminate the interiors.

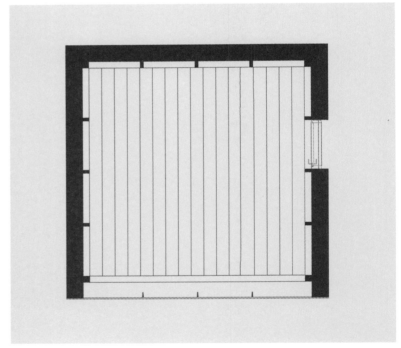

Inspired by the traditional A-frame cabin, Klein A45 functions as flexible and minimalist tiny house, while connecting the interior with the surrounding nature.

Arosa

The initial task for the Arosa maisonette was the clients' wish to optimize the floor plan while adding an extra bathroom with shower to the guest bedroom. Go Interiors was responsible for the whole interior design including the development of the material, lighting and furniture concept. The master bedroom is equipped with a reading nook and lounge area guaranteeing a high degree of personal comfort and relaxation. The attic has been transformed into a kids bedroom with four beds. Downstairs a separate dining area offers space to enjoy family life while its decorative wooden structure echos the charm of Alpine chalets. The extensive use of wood and high-quality materials creates a well-balanced mixture of traditional and contemporary lifestyle.

A modern reinterpretation of the Alpine chalet using wood as a characteristic feature.

Architect/designer: Austin Maynard Architects
Garden designer: Bush Projects

Location: Alphington, Victoria, Australia
Completion: 2014
Building type: house

Tower House

Tower House is a renovation and extension to a weatherboard home. The new design incorporates a studio, bedroom, bathroom, kitchen and dining room. The project creates a series of small structures of a scale and texture that do not dominate the context. Inspired by the sketches of the clients' twin boys the concept of an "anti-monolith" was developed assuring that the extension would not interfere with the building's original character. The exterior appears as a series of small structures, while internally the spaces and functions are large and connected. With a focus on the importance of communal exchange and interaction, a garden design has been developed that offers privacy and the opportunity to accommodate social gatherings, as required.

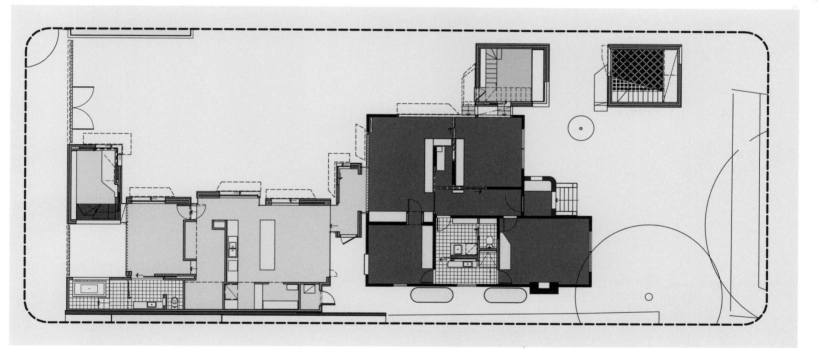

A series of small structures
provides a vertical living
concept that offers a high
degree of flexibility.

Architect/designer: Matteo Thun + Partners

Location: Rennweg, Austria
Completion: 2009
Building type: apartment towers

Edel:Weiss Residences

With local larch wood paneling and a biomass-based heating system, the apartment towers combine sustainability and contemporary living culture.

Built on the highest point of the Katschberg Alpine Pass, these two monolithic Edel:Weiss Residences apartment towers balance a respect for nature and tradition. Matteo Thun has created two vertical buildings in order to avoid the ongoing urban sprawl of this traditional winter sports area. The two cylindrical structures are clad with a lattice of local larch wood that symbolizes the direct association with the environment, fusing the inside and the exterior. Identical layouts built on different scales give all the apartments spectacular panoramic views of the natural landscape. Two different styles of décor offer a choice between a modern, urban flavor, or a more classic, traditional Alpine look. The entire complex is heated by the nearby power station, which supplies biomass energy.

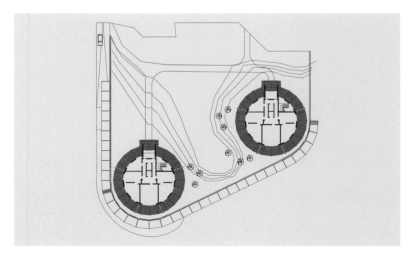

Architect/designer: Projectiles

Location: Epône, France
Completion: 2011
Building type: public building

Branched Offices

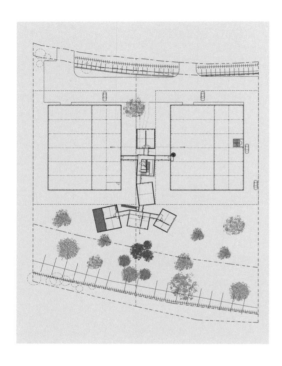

Projectiles were asked to create an office complex as an extension to a workshop and presented with two existing warehouses of 1,500 square meters situated 20 meters apart. The resulting extension has been introduced between these two volumes, joining them and branching out towards the far end of the parcel. The various volumes, linked by interior foot bridges, are constructed entirely out of wood and are perched four meters off the ground on top of an arrangement of roughly hewn beams. The complex is integrated within an arboretum of 20 trees of a dozen different species, offering blossom throughout the year.

The Branched Offices combine functionalism with a sustainable approach, while connecting the dwellings to the surrounding environment.

Architect/designer: koeberl doeringer architekten   Location: Gamlitz, Austria
Completion: 2015
Building type: cottage

Weingarthaus

Hans and Susanne Dreisiebner's Weingarthaus is located in the middle of their own vineyard. The exterior walls and ceilings are made of 20-centimeter-thick timber. Larch wood is used for all of the surfaces and treated with white pigmented oil on the interior walls. The virtues of timber allow for the floor and roof panels to overhang 2.5 meters on the southern side, creating a terrace and a canopy, the latter offering protection from the summer sun. All of the walls on the mountain side of the structure are made of concrete. Paying homage to the surrounding environment, the designers incorporated old grapevines, carefully crafted, into the exterior façade, giving the simple cubic structure an organic feel. The canopy above the terrace is also decorated on its underside with netting made of dried, backlit vines.

An extraordinary holiday domicile reflecting its environmental surroundings by means of architectural sophistication.

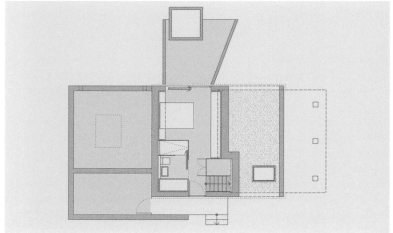

Architect/designer: Fabio Fantolino

Location: Courmayeur, Italy
Completion: 2014
Building type: mountain chalet

Courmayeur

Wood design in a warm and original character.

At the foot of Mont Blanc in Larzey, part of the small town of Courmayeur, an attic from a typical mountain house has been reinterpreted with clear and modern shapes through the use of distinctive choices of wood. The furnishings, walls, ceilings and floors, designed by Studio Fantolino, are defined by a recovered and selected ancient larch wood which gives comfort and a natural touch to the environment. Concrete support beams in the roof are left exposed to accentuate the visual contrasts between the old and the new. The living room, designed as a cohesive unit with the kitchen and dining area, is ornamented with works of art and various textiles, enabling the creation of intimate and comfortable zones. A reading area consists of a leather armchair that envelops the reader, whose book is illuminated by the soft light of the "Paw" lamp designed by architect Fabio Fantolino.

Architect/designer: Atelier Tekuto

Location: Chiba prefecture, Japan
Completion: 2012
Building type: residential building

Boundary House

This site is situated in an urban area between residential estates and farmland. The concept proposes a dramatic shift from economy-based to ecology-based lifestyle. The design was inspired by the idea of living under a tarp-like structure, where one can fully appreciate nature and move freely between inside and outside. The result was a maze-like composition where interior and exterior spaces are interwoven. A number of skylights were added, along with various plants that help to reinforce the interaction of nature and architecture. The exterior walls are finished with charred cedar wood, while the interior walls have been given a traditional wood finish. Both treatments have a similar character, once again reinforcing the connection between inside and outside.

Architect/designer: Markus Schietsch Architekten

Location: Zurich, Switzerland
Completion: 2014
Building type: elephant house

Elephant Park

The new elephant house at Zurich zoo is embedded in the extensive landscape of the newly designed Kaeng Krachan Elephant Park. The characteristic element is its striking wooden roof which blends into the landscape as a shallow free-form shell structure. The roof dissolves into a transparent maze-like structure that establishes an organic relationship to the surrounding forest. The continuously changing façade consists of lamellas that almost appear to be growing up towards the edge of the roof. The iconographic shell of the roof together with the dynamic façade form an atmospheric envelope and pictographic natural construction that concentrates the essence of the design into a symbiosis between architecture and landscape.

Architect/designer: stocker. dewes architekten

Location: Freiburg, Germany
Completion: 2012
Building type: passive house

From Stable to Passive House

The designers faced the challenge of transforming a former stable into a residential property complete with study. The final structure comprised living space for a three-person family and a home office along with the other necessary rooms. It is located on a site at the end of a valley and is surrounded by woodland. It was desired that the material chosen for the façade and roof should blend esthetically with the adjacent forest. The long, narrow form of the building allows the two distinct functions of the interior to emerge clearly. Passing through the entrance, the visitor encounters the office space, its walls as high as the building itself and the necessary work places integrated into a gallery level. The adjoining rooms are reached via the former feeding area, while the living space is located in the rear section of the building.

Architect/designer: SA Lab

Location: Saint Petersburg, Russia
Completion: 2019
Building type: tiny house

FLEXSE

FLEXSE is a sustainable stylish tiny house for city and countryside. The first prototype is a modern reinterpretation of a traditional Scandinavian grill house and a first prototype of a compact module. The design adapts to all weather conditions offering a cozy hideaway in winter and an open structure stretching over the terrace in summer. The first version of FLEXSE is used as a small barbecue house, though the structure might be used as a sauna, a guest house or a tiny house as well. In an urban context the module could be used as a small café, shop, or an office pod inside an existing building. The module can be assembled in parts on site and consists of 100 percent recyclable materials. The structure can be positioned on different foundations – concrete slab, metal piers, which allows to place it in the most remote areas, even on water.

A modern reinterpretation of the traditional Scandinavian grill house that combines sustainabilty with a high degree of flexibility.

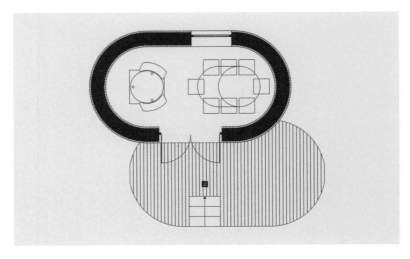

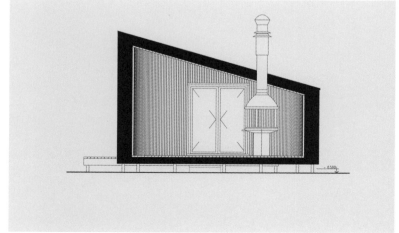

Architect/designer: Jacobsen Arquitetura

Location: Guarujá, Brazil
Completion: 2014
Building type: house

SM House

An architectural bridge between living space and nature's wilderness merging with the Atlantic Forest.

The designer's aim for this project was to create an elementary architectural composition combined with advanced techniques in wood housing construction. Located on São Paulo's northeastern shore, SM House was designed to be a beach house in its essence: a place of refuge in the middle of the Atlantic Forest, sheltered beneath porches from the rain and sun. It is a veranda house with large eaves and minimal walls where indoor and outdoor spaces are fully integrated. A transparent element was installed on the upper floor to ensure the visual relationship with the sea and the forest is preserved. This design creates a bright and open atmosphere that complements the successful merging of the complex with the surrounding environment. A flat roof with glued laminated timber and glass lateral closing was inserted where the living areas, kitchen and master suite are located. The veranda is set under a four-meter overhang and functions as an extension of the living room.

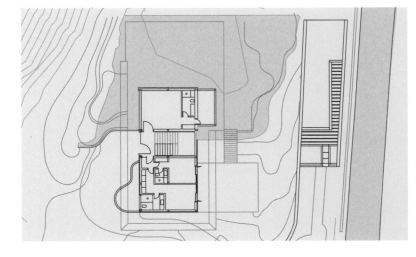

Architect/designer: juri troy architects

Location: Vienna, Austria
Completion: 2015
Building type: detached house

House with Cherry Tree

This small detached house was designed to be the principal residence of a married couple from Vienna. The block-like structure blends in perfectly with the surrounding architecture without compromising on character or esthetic distinctiveness. Due to the gently sloping nature of the site, the basement is exposed to the elements and becomes a key visual feature of the structure. The open-plan living space extends over five levels, its various spatial and design elements merging together to create an esthetically unified interior that exudes spaciousness despite the limited floor area. A wooden palisade wall ensures that the stairwell, which also functions as a library, remains visually connected with the adjacent spaces. The solid silver fir stairs double up as seats where the library's books can be read.

A cozy living environment impressing with simple forms and a warm atmosphere.

Architect/designer: Bohlin Cywinski Jackson

Location: San Francisco, CA, USA
Completion: 2016
Building type: café

Blue Bottle South Park

By resigning any ornated design features a clear and yet comfortable ambience has been created, functioning as a pragmatic frame for the subject of coffee brewing.

This new South Park location transforms the street-level storefront of a former Kohler warehouse into a light-filled, deliberately minimal interior space. The design of Blue Bottle South Park reveals the site's inherent beauty by stripping away the frivolous and unnecessary elements, elevating the most essential attributes of the architecture, such as original brick walls and heavy timber support columns, and enhancing the visible connection to the bustling SoMa streets. Upon entering the café, a lattice of floating wooden boxes greets customers, creating a series of shadows and sunlight throughout the space; bags of coffee and tableware available for purchase are nestled within the framework, creating an eye-catching merchandise display. A subdued palette of warm wood, pale blue walls and concrete flooring complements the company's branding and the craft of coffee making that is the hallmark of Blue Bottle.

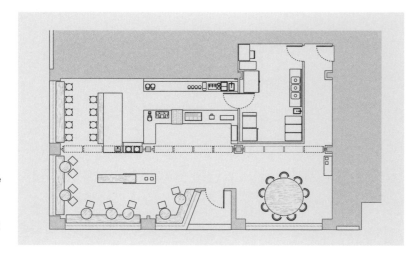

Architect/designer: Atelier Kristoffer Tejlgaard

Location: Aarhus, Denmark
Completion: 2016
Building type: installation

Dome of Visions 3.0

Defined by two geometries, the dome is part of a series of experiments focusing on the future use of wood and other sustainable materials.

Dome of Visions 3.0 is the third dome in a series of experiments and was built to test new ways of using wood and sustainable materials in the construction process. Its ephemeral nature renders it all the more unique. Most of the interior, plumbing, technical installations and solar cells were recycled from the first dome. The façade consists of two overlapping geometries: an exterior layer of polycarbonate and an interior layer of curved beams in wood assembled with simple laser cut steel. The mix of two geometries makes the dome more transparent and the construction more stable. The amount of material was reduced compared to earlier projects and production has been optimized, making the process of assembly easier and less energy-intensive. CLT (cross-laminated timber) was used for the house inside the dome, designed to accommodate residential uses and academic and cultural events. The CLT elements are modular and removable. The construction was virtualized and tested several times before production of the final elements.

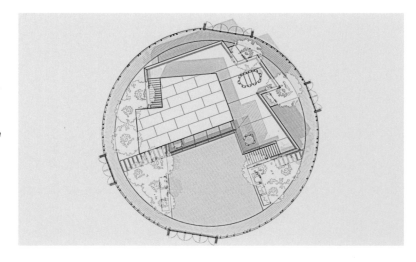

Architect/designer: Kauffmann Theilig & Partner

Location: Bad Wildbad, Germany
Completion: 2011
Building type: public spa

Outdoor Areas Palais Thermal

Kauffmann Theilig & Partner have realized this renovation and redesign of some terraces of the unused adjacent sanatorium for the use of the historic Palais Thermal in Bad Wildbad. The central feature is a wooden outdoor landscape with huge panorama decks and stairs. The elaborately folded surface integrates an existing sauna landscape on level one and an experience shower, two outdoor saunas, a sauna bar and a thermal pool with Jacuzzi, waterfall and massage jets on level two. The exterior cladding and façades are all covered with homogeneous wooden formwork. An atmospheric membrane construction protects from the view of the neighboring hotel and frames the view into the valley.

Architect/designer: Planungsbüro Jürgen Haller
and Peter Plattner

Location: Mellau, Austria
Completion: 2009
Building type: house

House Felder

Austrian shingle style blends tradition and nature within a primal setting.

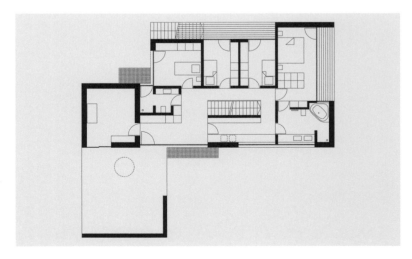

This house is located in a small village in the Bregenz Forest, at the foot of the famous 2,044-meter Kanisfluh massif. The two-story building is positioned on the outskirts of the built area away from other residences and has been seamlessly integrated into the natural surroundings. Local traditions served as inspiration during the planning process. The wooden detached house, clad in silver fir, harmonizes perfectly with the mountainous landscape of the Bregenz Forest, despite its distinctive, compact, cubic form. The upper story provides the building's most eye-catching architectural elements and houses the living and sleeping areas. An atmosphere of comfort and relaxation is generated by both the light-filled and gently slanting attic and the simple silver fir exterior cladding. The interior walls and furniture are finished in simple white precast elements that enable the creation of a relaxing, informal living space.

Architect/designer: Atelier Veloso Architects
(AVA Architects)

Location: Porto, Portugal
Completion: 2011
Building type: bar

La Bohème Entre Amis

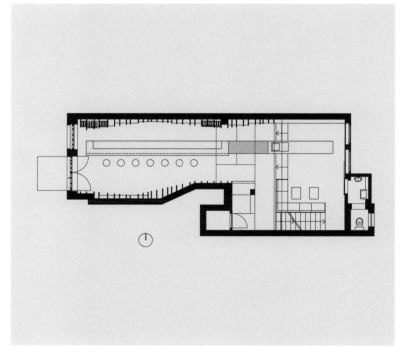

The bar La Bohème Entre Amis is located in the Galeria de Paris street, amidst the downtown area of Porto, and has been recently redesigned by AVA Architects. Changes made to the façade were solely at the level of framework and entrance span, combining an Afizélia wood (natural color) with colorless laminated glass. The bar spans three levels: the main floor, basement and a mezzanine. The bar counter is located on the main floor, next to the public entrance door. An existing wooden bar on the lower level was maintained and a large wine showcase added. The composition and design of the elements in the framework were formulated taking the interior space into account, while introducing rhythm by drawing vertical uprights.

Architect/designer: Elías Rizo Arquitectos

Location: Tapalpa, Mexico
Completion: 2015
Building type: house

Casa GG

An architectural promenade that seems to be born directly out of its natural environment.

The project for Casa GG emerged from a very particular commission. The client, a middle-aged bachelor, wanted to build a weekend house in the forest of his mountainous property in the state of Jalisco. The aim was to create an open relationship between the architectural spaces and the surrounding environment. The rugged topography was a determining factor in the layout of the project, which is designed on a series of terraces carved into the hill and linked by a zigzag path. The property is accessed from the highest point. The roof of the house, the first façade that confronts the visitor, is seen between the trees as an exposed concrete slab covered with gravel, and reveals the broken profile of the building. From the garage a staircase, made of rectangular stone slabs of differing dimensions, arises from a carpet of gravel, an esthetic echo of the roof that makes the building appear like an extrusion of the land itself.

Baumhaus Halden

A hideaway completely clad with oiled oak, creating an elegant but natural ambience.

The wish of both clients was to create a special hideaway for themselves and for guests. In addition, the future tree house is to provide a very pleasant environment for psychotherapeutic sessions. The small house in the trees is characterized by the living room and bedroom, which opens up to the gable. Only oiled oak was used to clad the walls, ceiling, floor and built-in furniture. This gives the interior a calm and elegant character. Above the integrated galley and bathroom there is a gallery with a comfortable sleeping area. A highlight of the bathroom is the washbasin made of natural stone, which was found in the nearby river. A small wood stove provides warmth and comfort on cold days.

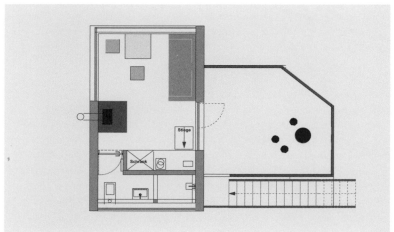

Architect/designer: Ateliers Jean Nouvel
Interior architect: Koichi Takada Architects

Location: Doha, Qatar
Completion: 2019
Building type: museum gift shop

National Museum of Qatar Gift Shops

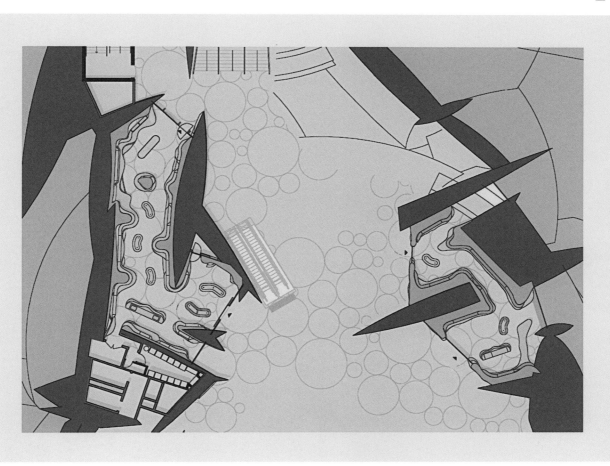

Located on a 140,000-square-meter site at the south end of Doha's Corniche, the National Museum of Qatar is the first landmark visible to travelers arriving from the airport. The exterior of the National Museum of Qatar was designed by French architect and Pritzker prize winner, Jean Nouvel. The interior design by Koichi Takada Architects reflects the Qatari history, while the forms and materials used aim to respect and complement Jean Nouvel's architecture. Inspired by rock formations and other desert scapes, the wooden installations echo the beginnings of the trade, nomadic lifestyle and beautiful natural environment. Being sculptural and organic alike, the design evolved to translate a story into a visual reflection and memorable experience.

Organic wooden forms echo the natural desert environment, thus reflecting the beginnings of the Qatari history.

Architect/designer: LINK arkitektur

Location: Fredrikstad, Norway
Completion: 2015
Building type: farmhouse

Øvre Tomtegate 7

A 19th century farmhouse was transformed into a contemporary living space without losing its traditional charm.

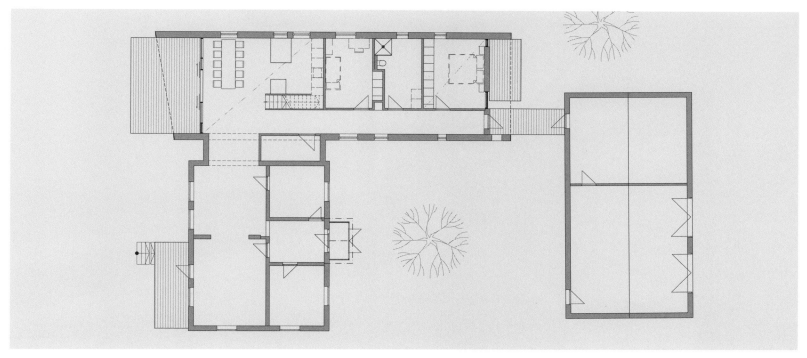

Inspired by the original 19th-century design, a rundown farmhouse on the east side of the Glomma River has been brought into the 21st century by LINK arkitektur. The new building design was heavily influenced by the traditional gable-roofed farmhouse. Glass and aluminum have been used extensively throughout. Both the roof and façade of the extension are clad with Kebony wood, chosen by the architects as it helped them to maintain the traditional style. Initially, Kebony cladding has a deep brown color – similar to that of tropical hardwoods – but when exposed to light and weathering over time the color of the wood softens to adopt a delicate silver-gray patina, perfectly in keeping with the light tones of the wood paneling on the inner walls.

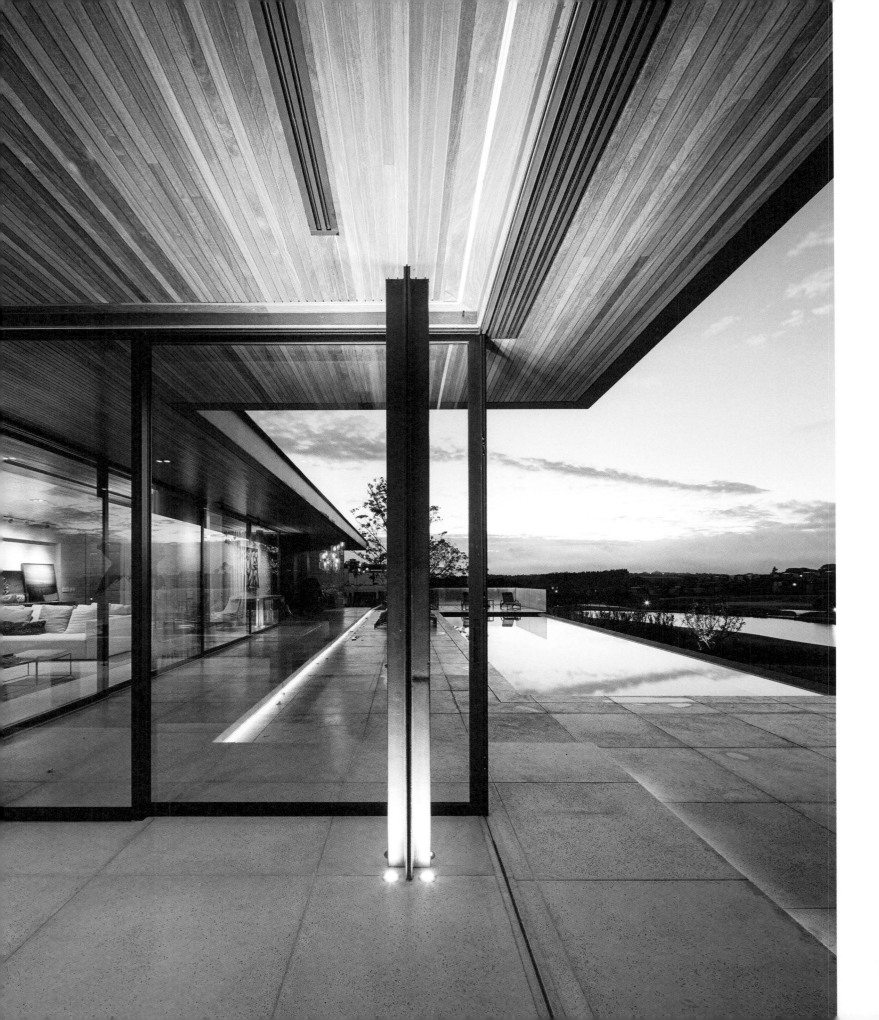

Architect/designer: Fernanda Marques
Arquitetos Associados

Location: São Paulo, Brazil
Completion: 2015
Building type: country house

Fazenda Boa Vista

In line with the owners' aspirations, a single vision guided the design and construction of this farmhouse in Porto Feliz, São Paulo: the creation of a country home that emphasizes its integration with the landscape, preferably by means of a lightweight structure, with large openings and glazed surfaces. Measuring 700 square meters, the steel-framed house follows the shape of the terrain. The façade is made from seamless sliding panes and the choice of wood, stone and glass as materials reaffirms the project's simplicity. At sunset the structure turns into a large light box reflected on the surface of the swimming pool. The home comprises two clear volumes: the primary volume houses the living area, kitchen and master suite, while the side volume comprises four guest suites.

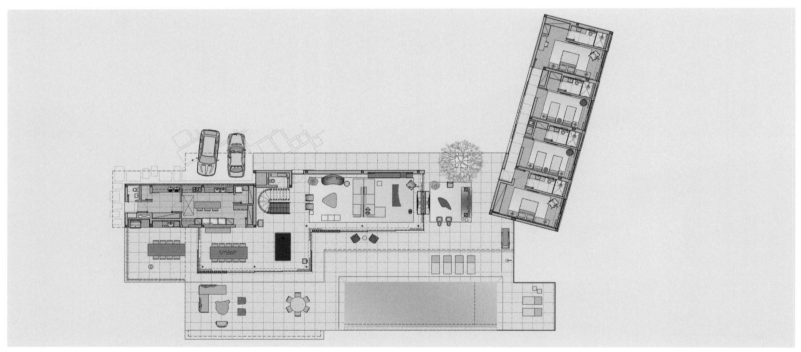

A private oasis of calmness
enlightening the countryside.

Architect/designer: Shinsuke Fujii Architects

Location: Yokohama, Japan
Completion: 2014
Building type: house with furniture system

Bookshelf House

The Bookshelf House was realized as a symbiosis between furniture system and interior design. By using a diagonal wall, a new, easy-to-use bookcase was created. Since all shelves of this furniture are inclined, the residents can easily reach the objects on the upper floors without the need for a ladder. In addition, books do not fall down when an earthquake occurs. The vertical side plate supports the structure, while the horizontal shelf supports the four-meter-long pillars. Not only as a piece of furniture, but also as an important aspect of interior design, the bookshelf functions as a sophisticated eye-catcher. With its soft wood tone, it blends harmoniously into the overall design.

A sophisticated furniture system that functions as symbiosis between functionalism and interior design.

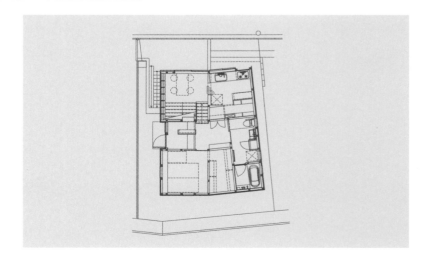

Architect/designer: DIA – Dittel Architekten

Location: Stuttgart, Germany
Completion: 2014
Building type: café

Pano Brot & Kaffee

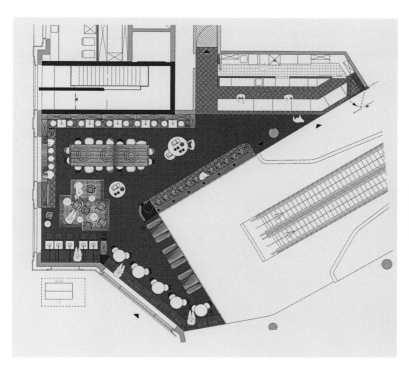

In the heart of Stuttgart DIA – Dittel Architekten have designed the city's first Pano Brot & Kaffee subsidiary. The café invites customers to enjoy handmade organic and locally sourced products in a comfortable and friendly atmosphere. Visitors of the café experience a harmonious, warm environment. The 225-square-meter room sports an unusual ceiling element that unfolds from the entrance towards the rear of the café. The use of high-quality materials, such as oak wood, hand-sewn real leather and Italian tiles, reflect the company's values: tradition, honesty and quality, making the Pano brand tangible.

Architects: Buero Wagner

Location: Munich, Germany
Completion: 2013
Building type: cocktail bar

Gamsei Cocktail Bar

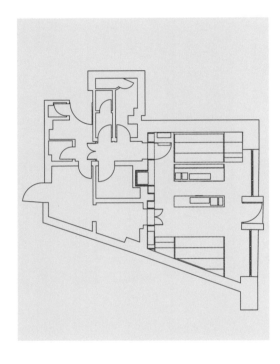

The Gamsei Cocktail Bar, built in 2013 in Munich, Germany, functions as an antithesis to the concept of globalization. All ingredients are produced locally. Buero Wagner has transformed this basic idea into a striking architectural language. An entirely new approach has been taken for the interior design. Two opposite benches, recalling the impression of the open structure of an amphitheater, blur the boundaries between the barkeeper and his guests. The storage space for ingredients forms part of the architectural concept, functioning as a pragmatic solution and unique design element. The individual bar elements have been freed of visual barriers and offer views of dried herbs and other elements. The interior design is completed with white ceramic vessels that hang down from the ceiling and contain self-made essences.

The architectural language expresses an antithetical statement to globalization.

Architect/designer: Baulhús

Location: Flateyri, Ísafjarðarbær, Iceland
Completion: in progress
Building type: house

Pedersen Residence

This abandoned house had been empty for 15 years when it caught Halfdan Pedersen's interest. The designer and his friends demolished and rebuilt it from ground up, using strictly reclaimed and salvaged materials from all over Iceland. All visible wooden elements, walls, floors and ceilings were personally collected by the architect throughout the country. Every door and every cabinet, sink, faucet, bathtub, radiator – and everything in between – was found, cleaned, restored, transported and assembled piece by piece, even the corrugated iron facing on the outer walls and roof. Following a sustainable approach, the massive recycling project has taken 13 years of careful and patient work and is still ongoing.

All visible wooden elements were collected by the architect, creating a living space determined by an extraordinary sense of individuality.

Index A–Z

A

Agricultural College Ritzlhof
Raimund Dickinger /
Mario Ramoni
→ p. 104

Arosa
Go Interiors
www.go-interiors.ch
→ p. 122

Atrevida House
Luz de Piedra
www.luzdepiedra.com
→ p. 78

B

Baumhaus Halden
baumraum
www.baumraum.de
→ p. 182

Blue Bottle South Park
Bohlin Cywinski Jackson
www.bcj.com
→ p. 162

Bookshelf House
Shinsuke Fujii Architects
www.fujiia.c.ooco.jp
→ p. 200

Boundary House
Atelier Tekuto
www.tekuto.com
→ p. 146

Boutique Intersybarite
sistémica
www.arquitecturasistemica.mx
→ p. 34

Branched Offices
Projectiles
www.project-iles.net
→ p. 136

C

Casa BGS
Alvaro Moragrega / Arquitecto
www.alvaromoragrega.com
→ p. 96

Casa Camar
Jachen Könz architetto
www.koenz.ch
→ p. 26

Casa GG
Elías Rizo Arquitectos
www.eliasrizo.com
→ p. 178

Casa Mororó
studio mk27
www.studiomk27.com.br
→ p. 64

Courmayeur
Fabio Fantolino
www.fabiofantolino.com
→ p. 144

D

Dome of Visions 3.0
Atelier Kristoffer Tejlgaard
www.atelierkristoffertejlgaard.com
→ p. 166

Don Café
Innarch
www.innarch.ch
→ p. 14

E

Edel:Weiss Residences
Matteo Thun + Partners
www.matteothun.com
→ p. 132

Elephant Park
Markus Schietsch Architekten
www.markusschietsch.com
→ p. 148

F

Far Pond
Bates Masi + Architects
www.batesmasi.com
→ p. 84

Fazenda Boa Vista
Fernanda Marques Arquitetos
Associados
www.fernandamarques.com.br
→ p. 196

Feisteinveien
Rever & Drage Architects
www.reverdrage.no
→ p. 82

FiftyThree, Inc.
+ADD
www.plusadd.org
→ p. 20

FLEXSE
SA Lab
www.salab.org
→ p. 150

From Stable to Passive House
stocker. dewes architekten
www.stocker-dewes.de
→ p. 149

G

Gamsei Cocktail Bar
Buero Wagner
www.buerowagner.eu
→ p. 210

Gottshalden
Rossetti + Wyss Architekten
www.rossetti-wyss.ch
→ p. 114

Grotto Sauna
Partisans
www.partisanprojects.com
→ p. 24

H

Holzschnitzerei Perathoner
bergmeisterwolf Architekten
www.bergmeisterwolf.it
→ p. 74

House Felder
Planungsbüro Jürgen Haller
and Peter Plattner
www.juergenhaller.at
→ p. 172

House Krokholmen
Tham & Videgård Arkitekter
www.thamvidegard.se
→ p. 48

House Refurbishment
in Kaga
Tailored design Lab.
www.tailored-design.com
→ p. 60

House with Cherry Tree
juri troy architects
www.juritroy.at
→ p. 158

K

K21 Skardsøya
Tyin Tegnestue Architects
www.tyinarchitects.com
→ p. 110

Kilden Performing
Arts Centre
ALA Architects
www.ala.fi
→ p. 70

Klein A45
BIG-Bjarke Ingels Group
www.big.dk
→ p. 118

L

Knoll Ridge Café
HB Architecture
www.hbarchitecture.co.nz
→ p. 52

La Bohème Entre Amis
Atelier Veloso Architects
(AVA Architects)
www.ava-architects.com
→ p. 176

La Galerie du Vin
OOS
www.oos.com
→ p. 56

Library in Proville
Tank architectes
www.tank.fr
→ p. 44

M

Mei Li Zhou Church
Tsushima Design Studio
www.tdstudio.jp
→ p. 100

Meier Road
Mork-Ulnes Architects/sfosl
www.morkulnes.com
→ p. 36

Modern Dandy
Goodnova Godiniaux with
Yulia Orlova
www.goodnova2.com
→ p. 40

Morerava Cottages
AATA Architects
www.aata.cl
→ p. 35

N

National Museum of Qatar
Gift Shops
Ateliers Jean Nouvel
www.jeannouvel.com
Koichi Takada Architects
www.koichitakada.com
→ p. 186

Nest
UID architects –
Keisuke Maeda
www.maeda-inc.jp/uid
→ p. 106

O

Outdoor Areas Palais Thermal
Kauffmann Theilig & Partner
www.ktp-architekten.de
→ p. 170

Knoll Ridge Café
HB Architecture
www.hbarchitecture.co.nz
→ p. 52

Øvre Tomtegate 7
LINK arkitektur
www.linkarkitektur.com
→ p. 192

P

Pano Brot & Kaffee
DIA – Dittel Architekten
www.di-a.de
→ p. 206

Pedersen Residence
Baulhús
www.baulhus.com
→ p. 214

R

Residence in Dusseldorf
Architekten Wannenmacher +
Möller
www.wannenmacher-moeller.de
→ p. 92

S

SM House
Jacobsen Arquitetura
www.jacobsenarquitetura.com
→ p. 154

Studhorse
Olson Kundig
www.olsonkundig.com
→ p. 8

T

Tower House
Austin Maynard Architects
www.maynardarchitects.com
→ p. 126

V

Vanke Triple V Gallery
MOD
www.modonline.com
→ p. 18

Vigoss R&D
Zemberek Design
www.zemberek.org
→ p. 88

V-Lodge
Reiulf Ramstad Arkitekter
www.reiulframstadtarchitects.com
→ p. 30

W

Weingarthaus
koeberl doeringer architekten
www.koeberl-doeringer.com
→ p. 140

Picture Credits

104–105
Markus Bstieler

106–109
Hiroshi Ueda, Kanagawa

110–113
Pasi Aalto
www.pasiaalto.com

114–117
Jürg Zimmermann, Zurich

118–121
Matthew Carbone

122–125
Go Interiors

126–131
Peter Bennetts

132–135
Jens Weber, Christian Wöckinger

136–139
Vincent Fillon

140
Michael Sazel

141
Georg Ott

142 m.
Michael Saze

142 a., b., 143
Georg Ott

144–145
Chiara Cadeddu, Turin

146–147
Sobajima, Toshihiro

148
Dominique Wehrli

149
Yohan Zerdoun

150–153
Ekaterina Titenko

154–157
Leonardo Finotti, São Paulo

158–161
juri troy architects

162–165
Matthew Millman

166
Jonathan Bisagni and
Atelier Kristoffer Tejlgaard

167
Helle Arensbak

168 a.
Helle Arensbak and
Atelier Kristoffer Tejlgaard

168 m., 169
Atelier Kristoffer Tejlgaard

170–171
Roland Halbe / Artur Images
www.rolandhalbe.eu

172–175
Albrecht Imanuel Schnabel, Rankweil

176–177
José Campos

178–181
Marcos García

182–185
Laura Fiorio

186–191
Tom Ferguson Photography,
Oscar Rialubin

192–195
Hundven-Clements Photography

196–199
Fernando Guerra

200–205
Teruaki Tsukui

206–209
Martin Baitinger

210
Jann Averwerser

211
PK Odessa

212
Jann Averwerser

213
PK Odessa

214–219
Mikael Lundblad, Stockholm

Imprint

ISBN 978-3-03768-250-0
© 2020 by Braun Publishing AG
www.braun-publishing.ch

1st edition 2020

Editor: Editorial office van Uffelen
Editorial staff and layout: Julia Heinemann
Masterlayout: KOSMOS – Visuelle
Kommunikation/Martin Denker
Reproduction: Bild1 Druck GmbH, Berlin

All of the information in this volume has been
compiled to the best of the editor's knowledge.
It is based on the information provided to the
publisher by the architects' and designers'
offices and excludes any liability. The publisher
assumes no responsibility for its accuracy or
completeness as well as copyright discrepan-
cies and refers to the specified sources (architects' and designers' offices). All rights to the
photographs are property of the photographer
(please refer to the picture credits).

Cover front (from left to right, from above to below):
Lukas Schaller; Reiulf Ramstad Arkitekter;
Tuomas Uusheimo; Jonathan Friedman/Partisans
Cover back: Jens Weber, Christian Wöckinger